LITERARY
STARBUCKS

LITERARY STARBUCKS

Fresh-Brewed, Half-Caf,
No-Whip Bookish Humor

JILL POSKANZER,
WILSON JOSEPHSON,
AND NORA KATZ

Illustrated by Harry Bliss

St. Martin's Griffin 🐾 New York

LITERARY STARBUCKS. Text copyright © 2016 by Jill Poskanzer, Wilson Josephson, and Nora Katz. Illustrations copyright © 2016 by Harry Bliss. All rights reserved. Printed in the United States of America. For information, address St. Martin's Press, 175 Fifth Avenue, New York, N.Y. 10010.

www.stmartins.com

Designed by Steven Seighman

Library of Congress Cataloging-in-Publication Data

Names: Poskanzer, Jill, author. | Katz, Nora, author. |
    Josephson, Wilson. | Bliss, Harry, 1964– illustrator.
Title: Literary Starbucks : fresh-brewed, half-caf, no-whip
    bookish humor / Jill Poskanzer, Wilson Josephson, and Nora
    Katz; illustrated by Harry Bliss.
Description: First edition | New York : St. Martin's Griffin, 2016.
Identifiers: LCCN 2016003703| ISBN 9781250096791 (paper over
    board) | ISBN 9781250096807 (e-book)
Subjects: LCSH: Coffee drinking Humor. | Authors—Humor.
Classification: LCC PN6231.C565 P67 2016 | DDC 818/.602—dc23
LC record available at http://lccn.loc.gov/2016003703

Our books may be purchased in bulk for promotional, educational, or business use. Please contact your local bookseller or the Macmillan Corporate and Premium Sales Department at 1-800-221-7945, extension 5442, or by e-mail at MacmillanSpecialMarkets@macmillan .com.

First Edition: August 2016

10   9   8   7   6   5   4   3   2   1

To Tim Raylor, for a since-forgotten comment in class that inspired everything to follow. Let this be one of many endeavors you inspire your students to create.

—JP

To parents who read to their children; to librarians everywhere.

—WJ

To Susan Reisinger-Becker, for Moby-Dick.

—NK

ACKNOWLEDGMENTS

We're incredibly grateful for our **publishing team**: Christopher Hermelin, agent extraordinaire, for championing the project from day one; Harry Bliss, for making the words come to life in front of our eyes; and Sylvan Creekmore and the team at St. Martin's, for tireless edits and e-mails and support. Thank you for being patient with us as we embarked on this adventure.

Thank you to amazing **Carleton professors and staff** who challenged us and made us better at academics, writing, and real life: especially Ben Allen, Lawrence Burnett, Kathy Evertz, Renata Fitzpatrick, Peter Balaam, Pierre Hecker, Susan Jaret McKinstry, Victoria Morse, Bill North, Susannah Ottaway, Greg Smith, Julia Strand, and Serena Zabin. Thanks especially to Tim Raylor for teaching the class in which Jill came up with the idea for the blog!

Jill Poskanzer is grateful she has more than forty-five seconds to thank everyone in her life, and that she won't be played offstage by dramatic music if she goes over the time limit. First and foremost, thanks to her mother and father, for always backing her writing projects with 100 percent enthusiasm—their support is nothing short of astounding. Thanks also to kid brother Craig, who, somehow, thinks his big sister is cool even after all of these years of proof of the opposite. His pride means more to her than anyone else's in the world. A big thanks and shout-out to Rachel Ruller and Therese Kaufman for penning a few of the early posts and getting the blog ball rolling (and thanks as well for *many* wonderful years of friendship from both of them). A big thank-you to the English department at Carleton College, all of whom are funny, supportive, and brilliant in equal measure, and who challenge their students just the right amount to inspire them to great lengths. Last, Jill would like to thank all of the friends she's accumulated throughout her twenty-three years of life—both people she's met in real life (special thanks to Howens, the greatest roommates she could ever have hoped to have, and the other three members of her comps group, all of whom are phenomenal writers that she is constantly surprised and inspired by) and the friends she's made online (special thanks to the Council—without that first Tumblr project, *Literary Starbucks* may very well not exist).

Wilson Josephson owes unending gratitude to his mother and father, without whom—for all sorts of reasons—he would not be the man he is today.

Nora Katz sends love and gratitude to wonderful 4th Burtonites for four years of laughter and amazing puns; Brian, Sara, and Bryce for being in her life since day one; Rome friends for spritz and ridiculous train rides; and the Tunk crew for a lifetime of laughter, conversation, and amazing post-hike mojitos. To Matt Shay, for *Little Women*. To the Anderson and Katz families, especially Dana, Emily, Brian, Molly, Grandma and Grandpa, Dolly, Ellen, Sharon & Alan, Sarah & Wayne, Martha & Randy, Richard & Cheryl, and Phil & Ellen. To Alex, Jordan, Alison, and Naomi, the best friends, cousins, and co-conspirators she could ever hope for. To Grandfather, who probably wouldn't have understood this book but who would have loved it anyway. To Cynde, her favorite poet, and to Vangie and Doie, her favorite lovers of great literature. Most of all, to Mom and Dad for being her cheerleaders and supporters every minute of her life. Thank you for raising her to be who she is and always giving her books for her birthday.

Of course, a big thanks from two-thirds of the authors goes to Intertwining Melodies for always bringing joy, sweet jams, and even sweeter calves. We *thought* we knew we were funny, and this proves it.

And to the people we forgot to thank—it's because we don't love you enough.

LITERARY
STARBUCKS

up

e.e. cummings   g   o   e   s

to the counter &orders
an icedvanillalatte
he

        sits.

                                        waits.

        onetwothreefourfive minutes
until the baristalady   w h i s t l e s   his name—
"how do you like your coffee, mr. poet?"

The baristas have been in the shop for three minutes when they hear a knock on the glass at the front of the store. Someone on the other side of the door has his forehead pressed against the glass, almost as though he'd be unable to stand on his own. Clearly he needs coffee. One of the braver baristas opens the door; **John Keats** enters.

John Keats orders a Venti iced caramel Frappuccino. He sits down at a table by himself, sighs dramatically, and doesn't drink it.

Eugene O'Neill goes up to the counter first thing in the morning and orders a black coffee.

Mary Oliver enters the Starbucks. A flock of birds follows her through the door. She orders a chocolate smoothie, but the barista can't hear her over the general chaos. There's a kingfisher diving into the iced coffee, wrens are using straws to construct nests, and a large goose has caught itself in the ceiling fan.

"I can't work under these conditions!" shouts the barista.

The din seems to die down just long enough for Oliver to reach across the counter and grasp the barista's hand. "It does not have to be good," she says earnestly. She takes her half-made smoothie to go, leaving Starbucks overrun with wildlife.

Rip Van Winkle enters, yawns, and tries to order a glazed donut. "Sir," says the barista, "this is a Starbucks. We don't really do donuts." Rip Van Winkle looks around, bemused. "It sure looks like Dunkin' Donuts," he says. "The only thing that's any different is the sign. . . ."

Nick Carraway enters, but instead of ordering something for himself, he leans on the edge of the counter and narrates what everyone else is ordering for the entire day.

Harper Lee comes in and orders a Grande cappuccino. She thinks it tastes great, and the other people in the shop seem to agree, so she never orders another drink again. When her family friend orders her a tall decaf fifty-five years later, no one believes it's really for Ms. Lee.

Elizabeth Bishop

The art of coffee isn't hard to master;
so many cups seem brewed with the intent
to be drunk that the cup is no disaster.

Drink coffee every day. Accept the fluster
Of early mornings, hours badly spent.
The art of coffee isn't hard to master.

Then practice drinking longer, drinking faster:
places, and names, and where it was you meant
to order. None of this will bring disaster.

I got up early once. And look! my last, or
next-to-last of three cupped coffees drank.
The art of coffee isn't hard to master.

I drank two lattes, lovely ones. And, vaster,
some flavored Venti cappuccinos spent.
I miss them, but it wasn't a disaster.

Even ordering now (the joking voice, a gesture
I love) I shan't have mumbled. It's evident
The art of coffee's not too hard to master
Though it may look like (WRITE it!) like disaster.

Marcel Proust orders a gallon of coffee. "But, sir!" cries the barista, "that'd take seven of our biggest cups!" He downs all seven without hesitation, and his feat is met with great applause by the other patrons.

One of the baristas notices that the espresso machine is making a weird noise. She ignores it.

Faramir does not love the iced coffee for its chill, nor the latte for its froth, nor the to-go cup for its convenience. He just really needs his caffeine fix.

Here is **A. A. Milne**, bumping up the stairs of the shop. Here is his tweed jacket, thrown over a chair. Here he is at the counter, ready to order a green tea with extra honey.

William Butler Yeats goes up to the counter and has a trained falcon order his coffee for him. "Do you want regular or decaf?" asks the barista. "What??" asks the falcon.

A. A. Milne sits down at a table in the corner. His son enters and begins playing with **Yeats**'s falcon. Milne takes notes.

It remains quiet. There are falcon droppings all over the floor of the shop, but the health inspector isn't coming until tomorrow.

Chinua Achebe comes in and orders strong tea and a scone. He picks up the scone and it crumbles in his hands. "Sorry," the barista says. "Things fall apart."

A. A. Milne asks Achebe if he'd like honey on his scone.

"Don't bother about the scone," says **Achebe**.

Haruki Murakami tries to order something off of Starbucks' secret menu. The notion that there might be a secret menu surprises the barista, who has never heard of such a thing. Murakami is disappointed, but not particularly surprised, and decides to order a glass of steamed milk with a squirt of cinnamon syrup. While waiting by the counter, he listens to the jazz coming through the speakers, taps his foot, and remembers when he used to run a coffee shop. That had been a good time. He is so distracted by the past that he doesn't notice when a small cat begins to lap up his order. He snaps out of his reverie and chases off the cat. Later in the day, he goes looking for the cat, hoping to make reparations. He never finds it.

Mary Ann Evans goes up to the counter and gives her name as **George Eliot.** Everyone in the Starbucks knows one another, and knows everything about the others. One has a secret, but it will not remain hidden for long, especially since **Nick Carraway** will share it with everyone who passes through the Starbucks. The Starbucks is where all the townsfolk come to gossip, and one cannot expect to keep entirely to oneself. Eliot's Venti chai tea latte arrives. By the time she gets home, everyone on her moderately endowed estate—including her prettier but less engaging sister—knows what she has ordered. The chai tea latte is a commentary on social hierarchy in small-town England, but it is tasteful.

Harry Potter goes up to the counter and orders a butterbeer latte because **Dumbledore** told him to, and he's pretty sure he can trust that guy.

Roald Dahl goes up to the counter and orders a Grande hot chocolate and a tall iced peach green tea. He offers the foxy barista a piece of gum. She takes it and promptly turns into a blueberry. He leaves the shop and walks down the street with his extraordinarily tall companion.

Frances Hodgson Burnett orders a small cup of coffee. The barista brusquely states that the espresso machine is broken. Burnett picks up the (extremely heavy) machine, and she wanders to the back of the Starbucks, despite the barista's protests. Burnett finds a small, iron door. She carries the sickly espresso machine through it and returns after a few weeks, the machine running just like new. The previously rude barista lights up with glee. The espresso machine joyfully produces several cappuccinos perfectly.

Jack London goes up to the counter with twelve sled dogs in tow. The barista shows him the door.

Farley Mowat bursts from his camouflage behind the counter, terrifying baristas and sending coffee in every direction. He runs for the door, determined to track **Jack London** through the wilderness.

Robert Frost comes into the shop and orders a tall pumpkin spice latte. He is so eager that he drains the latte in mere moments. The empty cup is even heavier than the full one had been. "Nothing gold can stay," he says sadly, and walks away into the crisp fall morning, nearly bumping into **John Knowles**. The look they exchange communicates a deep understanding of the loss of innocence, and the love of a New England summer.

John Knowles goes up to the counter and orders an iced cinnamon *dulce* latte, which is slightly different from the iced cinnamon *dolce* latte, but not different enough that everyone in the Starbucks doesn't know what drink he is REALLY talking about.

Thornton Wilder comes in whistlin' and orders a cup of coffee. It's the perfect temperature. He closes his eyes and thinks of mama's sunflowers. Life is too short, isn't it? We should all stand 'round in this Starbucks talkin' about the old days. Grover's Corners doesn't have one of these newfangled coffee shops. He's ready to go back.

Before he can depart, **John Knowles** starts sharing tales of his high school days with Wilder. However, Wilder thinks Knowles is coming off as slightly uppity, and takes his drink to go.

Shirley Jackson goes up to the counter, tipping her hat to Mr. **Thornton Wilder**. She orders a coffee on the rocks, a simple order with a twist.

Ayn Rand orders an espresso macchiato. "This establishment is the very epitome of capitalism, and for that we must recognize and applaud it," she says. "The free market is victorious every time someone orders a coffee. Big business is the cornerstone on which America was destined to thrive." Meanwhile, **Jonathan Swift** jokes with the barista about whether Starbucks would ever consider using the tiny hands of impoverished children to sort their coffee beans. Ayn Rand applauds him for his ingenuity. Everyone in the shop is a little concerned about her.

When **Rand** gets up to leave, she notices a black dot on the bottom of her coffee cup. "What does this mean?" she demands, holding it up. **Shirley Jackson** nods grimly at the rest of the patrons. "You know what to do," she says.

Louisa May Alcott enters, ducks, and orders a cup of jo.

John Locke goes up to the counter. "The usual?" asks the barista. He considers the menu for a moment. "Y'know what?" he says. "Let's start with a clean slate."

Cormac McCarthy goes up to the counter. He asks for coffee black and bitter. Because the world is black and bitter. The barista toils to complete his order. No matter how well a thing is done, death slow or quick will come to the doer. He is pleasantly surprised by the coffee. Unpleasantly surprised, because he knows that soon it will be gone and it will be him and the barista alone. Empty Starbucks, empty cup, empty cups. Empty world. Cormac does not believe in refills.

Edward Lear thinks **Cormac McCarthy** takes himself too seriously.

William Wordsworth orders a smoothie. It reminds him of a lake he visited once as a child. Then again, so do most things.

The March family strolls to the counter together.

Meg orders a Frappuccino. She is immediately fulfilled. She and the assistant manager get married on the spot.

Beth befriends the franchise owner, who gives her his old espresso machine. She learns how to craft a heartbreakingly delicious brew and shares cups of it with everyone who walks in the door, including a feverish family in the corner. Finally, when she is ready, she orders a simple and delicious cup of tea. She tells the barista to taste it while she slowly begins to walk away. "Aren't you going to drink this?" asks the barista. "No," says Beth, "I never imagined myself drinking tea at a place like this. All I ever wanted was a little bit of jo." As the barista takes another sip, Beth vanishes. Everyone is emotionally destroyed almost immediately.

Unable to process Beth's disappearance, **Jo** orders an incredibly intricate, complex, and stylish drink. It is her first time at Starbucks, after all, and she wants to please the crowd. The barista convinces her to order a drink that's more like what she's used to having at home. It is perfect.

Amy goes up to the counter and takes Jo's drink.

Marmee goes up to the counter and orders a small cup of coffee.

"Don't you want to order a drink for your husband?" asks the barista.

Marmee chuckles. "You know, for a while there I completely forgot that he existed," she says.

The Ancient Mariner

The Count of Monte Cristo enters the Starbucks. He sees them. **The March sisters**. The four people who ruined his reputation and had him unfairly imprisoned for years. He immediately begins plotting revenge against them. He also orders a caramel macchiato, giving his name as Dantès. He then grossly overpays for his drink; the barista gives him his coffee cup with "the Count of Monte Cristo" written on it instead.

Charles Dickens goes up to the counter and orders a cup of tea. He quickly finishes it and asks for more. He can't afford to pay for the refill. The barista drags him out into the street and sends him to the poorhouse, where he pines away for his lost love, who is married to another man. He works his fingers to the bone in a factory, eventually rising to the upper echelons of society. Ten years later, he walks into the same Starbucks and orders a cup of tea. When he asks for a refill, the barista gives it to him free of charge. He pays for it anyway.

Alice in Wonderland goes up to the counter and never gets around to ordering her caffè latte because she just will not shut up about her cat Dinah.

Arthur Miller orders a Venti coffee, no cream, no sugar. He sits down in the corner and drinks it slowly. By the time he's finished, he has failed as a husband, a father, a man, and an American.

Nick Carraway comments on this from his seat near the counter. **Miller** calls over to him, "You know, I feel a little persecuted."

Alex sips a steamed milk. He finds it deeply disappointing, but at least it doesn't make him nauseated.

Tom Bombadil gallivants up to the counter and tries to order a chai tea, which would undoubtedly add a lot of nuance and complexity to the Starbucks world. The barista ignores him.

Charlotte Perkins Gilman goes up to the counter by way of the perimeter of the walls of the Starbucks. She orders a caramel macchiato, steps over a fainting customer, and takes her drink.

1. Sweetness has an urgency; **Maggie Nelson** takes her tea with extra honey.

2. Maggie Nelson tells the man sitting at the table next to hers about the beekeepers in Alsace whose hives began producing blue honey a few years ago. That honey is just as sweet, but it is the shade of the night sky.

3. The honey turned blue when the bees began using waste from a nearby M&M'S factory as food. The dyes passed through the bees' bodies and transformed from waste product into unique nectar, sweet and miraculous.

4. At the table next to Maggie Nelson, **Charlotte Perkins Gilman** is unimpressed. She's always preferred plain yellow honey, anyway.

F. Scott Fitzgerald orders a Grande coffee. He adds cream and sugar, but when he drinks it, it tastes more bitter than he expected. He drinks it all anyway.

Ernest Hemingway orders a black coffee. He adds nothing. He is a man, and he knows the truth of life. Its bitterness cannot be masked. The coffee reminds him of war—short but painful, swallowed down quickly. One could order worse drinks. Why did the Fitzgeralds make him get up so early?

Zelda Fitzgerald orders a drink all by herself. Her husband and Ernest Hemingway panic and have her removed from the Starbucks. The barista picks up her drink and tastes it. It is delicious.

Douglas Adams goes up to the counter and orders an Earl Grey. The barista turns a handle and there is a whirring that fills the entire coffee shop, followed by the screech of fingernails on a blackboard and something that sounds suspiciously like the theme from *Scooby-Doo!* It is the barista's first day, and she has already been mistaken once for a barrister and once for J. S. Bach, so she (quite bravely) accepts that maybe strange things just happen in this particular Starbucks. A mucusy batter flows reluctantly from the faucet, which was meant only to supply hot water. She shrugs, and hands it to Adams. He shrugs, and drinks it.

Sylvia Plath enters, bringing with her a stiff autumnal breeze that hints of winter. She decides to order a strawberry Frappuccino. On the other side of the window, fiery leaves have begun to fall. The leaves are too red; they remind her of beetles, of darkness, of the taut skin of the dead. The taste of strawberries turns thick and sour.

Hemingway has watched her since she came in, totally entranced. "Now that," he says to **Fitzgerald**, "is a woman who understands the brutality of life!" When he finally works up the nerve to speak to her, he opens with: "Could I interest you in my clean, well-lighted place?" Plath just stares at him until he leaves Starbucks.

James Baldwin sneaks behind the counter and writes "RaceTogether" on every cup.

Nabokov walks up to the counter and orders a shaken sweet tea in Russian, but asks if they have it in a kiddie size. The barista writes his drink order and name on the cup in English and hands it to him. When he reaches into his pockets to produce change, butterflies spill out, dashing themselves against the windows of the Starbucks. He does not finish drinking his tea; the barista decides not to throw it away and leaves it on the table long after all the other patrons of the Starbucks have left.

Hamlet

D'Artagnan orders an espresso. **Don Quixote,** immediately behind him in line, tells the barista he wants something worthy of a knight: "The drink," Quixote says, "must not be too sweet, for the tribulations of knighthood are many. Neither can it be too bitter, since knights work tirelessly to make the world a sweeter place. Most important, madam, my beverage must contain a dose of caffeine, for nobility without vigor is nobility wasted."

D'Artagnan, thinking he is being mocked and that this knight means to impugn his honor, casts down his gage. Quixote accepts: "Foils!" he exclaims, "at noon!" *Well, shit,* thinks d'Artagnan. "Any chance we could push that back a bit?"

While the men argue, the barista makes them both tall coffees with cream. Don Quixote is elated.

Wilfred Owen orders a caramel macchiato, which is what he heard Keats ordered when he was at Starbucks. He drinks half of it, but has to leave before he can finish. **Siegfried Sassoon** finishes his drink for him.

Vladimir and **Estragon** enter, but they don't order anything. They're supposed to meet someone here in just a few minutes.

Tim O'Brien orders a drink he calls the "Epistemic Frappe." The barista double-checks the menu. "I'm sorry, sir," she says, "but that's not a real drink."

"How can you know what's not real?" O'Brien asks.

He seems to pull a microphone from thin air and, with his lips a little too close to the mic, he tells everyone in the Starbucks that they've just had their minds blown.

Eugene O'Neill is still inside the shop. He is in the midst of his second confrontation of the day with another patron.

Virginia Woolf is exhausted by the man who has accosted her before she is even able to order. She walks up to the counter and orders a cup of lukewarm tea. The barista is beautiful. Woolf is married. What if everything had turned out differently?

Kate Chopin comes in and orders peach tea. The barista gives Chopin her change and their hands touch. Her face flushes. Is it hot in this Starbucks or is it just her? A piano plays. She contemplates her womanhood. She takes a single sip of the tea and grabs Virginia Woolf's hand, and they run out of the shop toward the ocean.

Neil Gaiman goes up to the counter and orders a salted caramel mocha. While waiting for his order, Gaiman begins a conversation with an elderly woman sitting by the window. She weaves for him a long story, filled with deep shadows and monsters he never knew he feared. The protagonist seems more and more familiar as the story progresses. The barista interrupts the story, calling: "Mocha for Gaiman!"

"I'll be right back!" Gaiman exclaims, as he dashes off to get his order. But by the time he returns to the table by the window, the old woman has disappeared, leaving only a faint odor—something between the dark woods of November and the aging pages of a well-worn book.

Toni Morrison goes up to the counter and places her order, which is so novel that Starbucks immediately adds it to their menu. Twenty-seven years later, Morrison orders the drink again; she is pleasantly surprised to find that it might be even better than everyone has said.

John le Carré orders a small coffee with sugar, but no cream. As he orders, he winks at the barista. She nods and hands him a manila envelope with his order.

Thomas Pynchon goes up to the counter and orders a short dark roast. They call his name, and he flees the scene.

John le Carré attempts to tail Pynchon. He thinks he's being stealthy. Soon, he finds he's struggling to determine what is conspiracy and what is just his imagination.

Benedick and Beatrice arrive separately and end up next to each other in line, to their disappointment. The barista tells each of them their drink has been paid for by the other.

BEN: Did you not order this for me?

BEA: Why, no.

BEN: Well, then the barista has been deceived, they swore you did.

BEA: Did you not order this for me?

BEN: Troth, no.

BEA: Well, then the barista has been deceived, they swore you did.

BEN: They swore you were near sick waiting here for me.

BEA: They swore you were near dead waiting for me!

BARISTA: Here's two orders, each written in the other's hand, to pay for each of your drinks.

BEN: A miracle! Here's our own hands against our drinks. Come, I will pay for your coffee, but only because I suspect you cannot pay for it yourself.

BEA: I would not deny you, but only to save your life, for I was told you were in a consumption.

BEN: Peace! I will stop your mouth.

[he hands her the coffee; she drinks]

You go up to the counter. You need a glossy hard-cover, one that you think will look good on your coffee table, one that you think will earn you a few chuckles from houseguests. Starbucks has just the thing! You take the book to a corner table, content—buying things always appeases ennui—and you begin to flip through your new book. You begin to think you may have overpaid.

Thorin Oakenshield goes up to the counter and orders a Venti coffee with whipped cream. It's been a long time since he's had this drink. He's not entirely sure what's inside. All he knows is that he wants it with every fiber of his being. The barista makes the drink quickly but fears what will happen to Thorin when he drinks it. The barista sneaks out from behind the counter and gives the drink to the tall blond man in the corner before sprinting away. It's better this way. Right?

Jean Valjean goes up to the counter and orders a tall black coffee without cream or sugar. On his way out, he surreptitiously slips a scone into his jacket pocket. The barista vows to spend the rest of his life trying to find him. Thorin likes that guy and his extremely reasonable reaction to petty theft.

Michel Foucault goes up to the counter and orders an iced coffee. Is his choice a product of his past or his present? Aren't we all just at the whim of the power structures that control our society? Should we abandon this Starbucks and take control of our own beverages? What do we know about coffee? What do any of us know about anything? The barista, not surprisingly, quits his job and goes to live with Thorin on a mountain.

Elizabeth Barrett Browning goes up to the counter. The barista begins to speak to her in perfect meter, asking what she'd like to drink. Not missing a beat, she responds:

"How do I take my coffee? Let me count the
    ways.
With cream and sugar, syrups, foam, milk—light.
You never reach the bottom with a Trenta's
    height,
For the ends of Frappuccinos ne'er have Grace.
I take it in the morning with the rays
Of that great sun, and drink 'til full daylight.
I take it freely, as men strive for Right;
I take it purely, as they turn from Praise.
I take it with Passion put to use
In Tazo teas, and with my childhood's faith.
I take it rapidly and never lose
A single drop,—I take it with the breath,
Smiles, tears, of all baristas!—and, if God choose,
I would drink coffee daily until death."

Moments later, barista and customer join hands and run off to Italy together. This turns out not to be a great career move for the barista, because he can't find a single Starbucks anywhere.

Dr. Seuss cheerfully goes up to the counter.

He orders a frosty fluff iced tea flan flouter.

He stays very still

His drink remains chilled

He waits (very patient) for his cup to be filled.

He calls to the shop, "I speak for the teas, for the teas have no tongues.

"And I'm asking you, sir, at the top of my lungs,

"Why is my cup taking so long to fill?

"I've been standing here, waiting, with my five-dollar bill."

And finally, after a long, quiet pause,

He lets out a series of hearty guffaws.

"I'm sorry, good sir,"

He cries out with a smile,

"It's totally fine my drink's taking a while.

"I'll stand here and read, wearing nothing but tweed,

"And I know that my drink will be done with great speed."

He stands and he waits,

And he waits,

And he waits,

And finally, now it's a quarter to eight,

He hears the barista call out, "Theodore!"

Dr. Seuss stands up and goes for the door.

The barista calls out, "Good sir, here's your
drink!"

Dr. Seuss turns around and tries hard to think.

"I'm so sorry again," he says with a smile,

"It's just I'd forgotten my surname was Geisel."

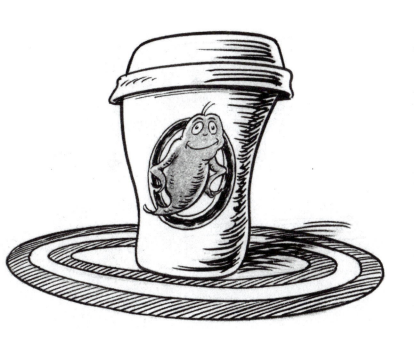

Harlan Ellison is denied service. "Sorry, sir," says the barista. "No dogs allowed." The man and his dog go outside and plot their revenge.

The Lyric "I" orders a small hot chocolate and, unable to find anywhere else to sit, asks to share a table with **You.** I does not disturb You as You read.

Rumi says he will never understand
The coffee addiction found in this land.
"It's just a drink," he says haughtily.
"I'm sure it won't have this effect on me!"
But lo, one sip, and he's converted.
If only with Starbucks he'd never have flirted!

Samuel Taylor Coleridge stares at the menu, lost in thought. Just as the light of a thought breaks through his clouded conscious—just as an order begins to coalesce—**Oscar Wilde** bumps into him. Coleridge finds he can remember nothing; he storms out.

Oscar Wilde orders a Grande hot chocolate and a muffin for his invalid friend **Bunbury**. The barista asks him if he is ordering in earnest. No one picks up the drink.

Cordelia goes up to the counter. "What would you like today?" asks the barista. "Nothing," she says.

Daisy Buchanan goes up to the counter and orders the drink society expects and has pressured her into ordering. Everyone hates her for it anyway.

Daisy Miller orders an espresso. "Careful now," the barista says, "this is very hot." She laughs and downs it in one big gulp, making deliberate eye contact with the barista the whole time. Predictably, she burns her throat horribly. As medics arrive, she lets out a weak laugh and says: "That's all I wanted—a little fuss!"

The Daisys take a corner table together and continue to buy Frappuccinos throughout the day.

Homer enters the Starbucks and asks if they have any wine dark teas. The barista goes into the back to check. He doesn't return for twenty years.

Virgil comes in and orders a Venti cappuccino. He goes to sit at a table, but sees another toga-clad man sitting in his usual seat.

"Excuse me, but I usually sit here," says Virgil.

"Oh, you do?" says the man, as he turns around.

"Oh, hey, Homer," says Virgil.

"I was sitting here first," says Homer.

"I know, but—"

"No buts, kid," says Homer. "And give me that cappuccino."

Virgil leaves the store, deciding then and there that he can definitely find another Starbucks just as good as this one on the other side of town.

As the day turns into afternoon, the baristas feel as if the work has gotten harder. None of them realize they are missing a staff member.

When the barista asks **Raskolnikov** what he would like, he sweats, shakes, and faints.

Edgar Allan Poe goes up to the counter and orders a coffee. For the next two hundred years, everyone argues over exactly what it is he ordered; they can't agree, all they know for sure was that he definitely ordered something.

John Milton orders a Venti Caramel Ribbon Crunch Frappuccino blended coffee. "It smells like Paradise," he breathes as he picks it up off the counter. He drops it immediately.

Aristophanes goes up to the counter followed by a horde of twenty masked men. They speak his order in unison. This is, apparently, the only way he is capable of communicating anything.

Amelia Bedelia goes up to the counter and orders a flat white. The barista hands her a cup of coffee.

"What is this?" she asks, irritated. "I just wanted a piece of paper."

Walt Whitman comes into the Starbucks and greets **The Lyric "I"** like an old friend. He orders a green tea. Whitman would like to sip it as he rejoices in the clamor of mankind, but **Patricia Lockwood** is actually making him pretty uncomfortable with the way she keeps trying to look down his shirt.

Whitman climbs up the fire escape to the roof and sounds his barbaric yawp. A bell tolls. **Allen Ginsberg** sits up in his seat. "Something horrible has happened."

Allen Ginsberg goes up to the counter and says, "Coffee. God damn it, coffee."

The drink will cost three dollars and twenty-eight cents and there is no more cream left in the jug.

He walks out under the trees and there is a guitarist in the street playing a tune in the moonlight.

Ginsberg is young and we are young and the streetlights flicker and go out and the supermarket down the street has no more peaches.

It is summer in California and the lukewarm breast of midnight has just started moving down the street.

Ginsberg looks up and breathes in the heavy air and smiles the deep smile of memory and baristas who never loved us and the drops of cream left on the counter.

Walt Whitman is dead.
The coffee is cold.

Orpheus goes up to the counter and orders a Green Tea Crème Frappuccino. He hangs around the counter, inadvertently forcing **Nick Carraway** to move aside. The barista tells him he can go sit down, she'll call his name when it's ready, and that he shouldn't hover or watch her make it. He walks away. When the barista turns back around, she realizes that he's actually just ducked under the counter and is surreptitiously watching her. She asks him to leave the premises. He doesn't get to drink his coffee.

The Lyric "I" is really awfully sad about this whole Walt Whitman business, and in such close quarters it's impossible for **You** to pretend you haven't noticed. You go up to the counter and buy two small hot chocolates.

Chuck Palahniuk goes up to the counter and orders a coffee. The barista has a black eye. He nods formally to Palahniuk, who takes his coffee to go and leaves in a hurry, bumping straight into **Brett Easton Ellis.** His coffee spills all over the latter, who glares at Palahniuk as he quickly rounds the corner.

Brett Easton Ellis and **Donna Tartt** enter Starbucks. **Ellis**, drenched in coffee, goes up to the counter and orders a cappuccino. Despite his having ordered drinks from Starbucks before, the barista balks a little at Ellis's choice to order a cappuccino, and refuses him service. Ellis sits down at a table as various other patrons in the shop begin to argue about whether or not his order was a self-aware act or just a bad decision of the time. He and Tartt whisper quietly to each other in a language that sounds unfamiliar to others, ignoring attempts from various patrons to speak with them. Eventually, everyone comes to the conclusion that it was a very fine drink to order, and at last Ellis goes back up to the counter. Of course, his ordering at Starbucks is meant to be read as an ironic indictment of capitalism. They leave the Starbucks, but not before Tartt sneaks a caramel macchiato under her arm without paying for it. One single patron notices this act. It is the only story he will ever be able to tell.

Ralph Waldo Emerson enters Starbucks and orders two Venti Americanos for him and his wife. His wife hints to **Henry David Thoreau**, who has accompanied them against their wishes, that she wants him to sit at a separate table, but he is incredibly dense and loudly drags a chair over to join the Emersons.

Henry David Thoreau goes up to the counter and begins describing the perfect cup of coffee that everyone in modern civilization should enjoy. He finds himself unable to pay and storms out angrily. Five minutes later his aunt comes in and pays for it. Afterward, he makes the Emersons pay for his laundry at the Laundromat.

Thoreau claims that he can't live without his early morning coffee.

"It's two P.M.," says a barista.

Konstantin Levin wants nothing more than he wants to join the laboring baristas behind the counter. He sneaks into a green apron and begins working alongside the baristas. The incessant, nearly mechanical work strikes him as beautiful, in its own way. An inner peace swells inside him.

Dante enters Starbucks and orders a caramel Frappuccino. However, he doesn't have enough money to pay for it. He needs to walk nine whole blocks to his friend Virgil's house, borrow the change, and come back before he can finally get his coffee.

Sartre orders a black coffee. He accidentally picks up Dante's order and drinks it instead. He spits it out. "Hell is other people's coffee," he says.

Susan Pevensie goes up to the counter, but the barista won't let her order any coffee because she is wearing lipstick.

Daisy Buchanan invites **Susan** over to sit with her and **Daisy Miller**. "We girls have to stick together," she says.

"Fuck lines!" yells **Steve Roggenbuck**. "Fuck!"

"Um," says the barista, "would you like to order anything?"

"Yes! YOLO!" He is still shouting. "I'll take one of everything!"

He turns and looks directly into the camera. "It's all so beautiful," he whispers.

The barista decides that he probably doesn't actually want one of everything, and instead sells him a scone from the display case. He is disproportionately grateful.

Holden Caulfield goes up to the counter to order a dark roast, but he's forgotten all his money at home, so his little sister has to pay for it. He stares moodily out the window as he waits for it to brew, wondering where the ducks in the pond across the street go in the winter. Also, he's pretty sure the barista is a phony.

Adrienne Rich

First having read the menu,
and loaded the coffee grounds,
and checked the machine,
she put on
the apron of green fabric
the absurd name tag
the grave and awkward mask.
She is having to do this
not like the baristas with their
assiduous chatter
within the sun-flooded Starbucks
but here alone.

There is a coffee.
The coffee is always here,
sitting innocently
close to the edge of the counter.
We know who it is for,
we who have drunk it.
Otherwise
it is a piece of morning cardboard
some caffeinated equipment.

She drinks it down.
Gulp after gulp and still
The coffee immerses her;
the green light
the oaky taste
of our human fuel.
She drinks it down.
Her breathing cripples her.
She gasps like a fish from the bottom of the cup
and there is no one
to tell her when the drink
will end.

First the coffee is brown and then
it is browner and then it is black and then
black because she is blacking out and yet
her drink is powerful,
it pumps her blood with power.
The coffee is another story;
the coffee is not a question of power.
She has to learn alone
to turn her body without force
in the deep dregs.

And now: it is easy to forget
what she came for
among so many who have always
lived here
drinking their caffeinated drinks
between the tables
and besides
you breathe differently in here.

She came to explore the Starbucks.
The drinks are purposes.
The drinks are maps.
She came to see the damage that was done
and the treasures that prevail.
She strokes the cup
slowly along the side;
it's something more permanent
than grounds or cream.

The thing she came for:
the Starbucks and not the story of the Starbucks
the thing itself and not the myth
the drowned face always staring
toward the outside
the evidence of damage
worn by customers into this threadbare shop
the edges of the Starbucks
curving their assertion
among the tentative haunters.

This is the place.
And she is here, the mermaid whose dark hair
streams green, the mermaid in her circular prison.
We circle silently
about the shop
we dive into the masses.
She is she; she is we.

The drowned face sleeps with open eyes
whose hair still bears the stress
whose green and white cargo lies
obscurely inside cups
clutched in hands and left on tables.

We are the half-destroyed instruments
that once held to a course
blinked sleep from our eyes
and drank.

We are, she is, you are
by hunger or thirst
the one who finds her way
back to this shop
carrying a cup, a drink
a menu
on which
her name does not appear.

The barista immediately recognizes **Suzanne Collins** and asks her to autograph his copy of *The Hunger Games*. When the hullabaloo dies down, **Ralph Ellison** comes over to her. "That must be nice," he says.

"I don't know. I wish more people recognized me for my earlier books."

"You had earlier books?" he asks.

Suzanne Collins shrugs. "Yeah," she says, "but they were sort of an underground thing."

William Golding orders an espresso. He collects his drink, but a rowdy group of boys rushes past him, knocking it to the ground. The espresso cup shatters.

Fagin goes up to the counter and orders thirty tall hot chocolates. Fagin pays for the drinks using a crisp one-hundred-pound note. The barista watches him leave and then puts his hand into his pocket, only to find that his wallet is gone. He runs out to the street, only to see Fagin wave at him cheerfully and then disappear around a corner, tailed by the group of rowdy boys.

Tom Sawyer goes up to the counter, but convinces a boy significantly less clever than himself to order his drink for him while he lounges by the window.

After delivering **Tom** his drink, **Oliver Twist** orders a gingerbread latte. He drinks it all quickly, goes up to the counter, and says "Please sir, may I have some more?"

"Um," says the barista, "we don't do free refills here, kid."

The baristas wonder why no one is bringing money into what is clearly a business.

Frank Herbert goes up to the counter and orders a vanilla spice latte. It's not quite what he was expecting.

Mark Twain orders the quintessential American coffee, but under a fake name. He leaves it there. No one is allowed to drink it for 100 years after he leaves.

Langston Hughes goes up to the counter
Says he likes his coffee black
Hughes goes up to the counter
'nough caffeine for a heart attack

Hughes goes up to the counter
Our barista's a little confused
She sees Hughes comin' up to the counter
Wants to know why he's singin' the blues

You're a famous poet, she says
As she leads him to a booth
Fame don't leave you no reason for bluesin'
And he moans: Lord, ain't that the truth!

Antoine de Saint-Exupéry goes up to the counter and sees that his barista is a grown-up. That is unfortunate, because grown-ups do not understand anything unless it is explained to them very clearly. He asks for a cup of coffee that's sweet but not too sweet. The barista doesn't understand his order. He is not surprised. A very small barista appears behind the counter and makes his coffee for him without missing a beat. They have a long conversation. Saint-Exupéry thinks he understands things a little bit better now. The small barista disappears.

Junot Díaz lays down newspapers before walking up to the counter. He orders three drinks: what he would have ordered as a child, what he would have ordered as a young man, and what he likes to drink now. When asked, he gives his name as Yunior.

Icarus goes up to the counter and orders a brewed tea. He downs it in a single gulp, burning himself.

"Maybe we're making the coffee too hot," says one barista.

Emily Dickinson goes up to the counter and stands there in complete silence before quietly ordering a cup of tea. When the barista asks for her name, she says, "I'm nobody. Who are you?" Amherst claims this took place in their onsite Starbucks.

José Saramago goes up to the counter. What would you like, he's asked, but in line he has been considering the people in Starbucks and not its menu, so he doesn't know, and he says as much, I don't know, which frustrates the barista. Then please go to the back of the line and we'll try again, Yes, I'm sorry, we'll try again. After a few moments, he knows what he wants, but now he must wait in line again, and the waiting is worse this time, since he now knows what he's waiting for. He distracts himself by making up lives for the people around him: He's a carpenter, She's a boxer, That one has never seen snowfall before. He returns to the counter, looks the barista in the eye, and finds his mind is blank. Right, he says, and leaves the counter, leaves the barista, leaves the Starbucks. He takes only the made-up lives of his fellow patrons; he is hardly empty-handed.

When the barista asks **Joan Didion** how her day is going, her answer is honest. This surprises, and perhaps even scares, the barista.

While waiting in line, **E. B. White** realizes that this is the same Starbucks his father used to take him to as a child. He is filled with happy memories, but as he sips his iced coffee, suddenly he feels the chill of death. It passes. Perhaps it was only a brain freeze.

Maya Angelou enters and orders seven different drinks—teas, coffees, juices, Frappuccinos—and a chicken salad sandwich. She sits down in the corner and begins chatting amicably with each customer. One leaves having met a singer, another a poet, another a diplomat—and so on, for hours, until the barista has to close down the shop. The customers gather on the street after Angelou leaves, all unconvinced that they were all talking to the same person.

George Orwell goes up to the counter, looks around suspiciously, and leaves. He only drinks coffee from independent shops.

Ray Bradbury orders a Grande coffee, black. He drinks it too quickly. "Be careful, sir!" the barista warns. "Two people have burned themselves already today."

"It was a pleasure to burn," replies Bradbury.

"Oh," says the barista. "You're talking about censorship!" Bradbury is furious about being misinterpreted and storms out of the Starbucks, leaving his drink on the counter.

Frodo Baggins tries and fails to order a cup of tea. **Samwise**, who is accompanying him, says, "Master Frodo will have a Grande green tea with room for cream, please." The barista hands the cup to Frodo, and the entire shop cheers. "Huzzah!" they cry. "Look at Frodo Baggins, ordering that cup of tea all by himself!" Later, Sam puts out a fire in the kitchen and Frodo is given the Presidential Medal of Freedom.

Sméagol goes up to the counter and—

No, no we mustn't go, precious.

We'll just order a chai latte, that certainly can't do any harm.

No, precious, no, they takes it from us.

Our money? Yeah, of course, this is a business.

They takes it from us and they puts it in their boxes.

No, no, but we want our coffee!

Gollum, Gollum, Gollum.

They sells us the coffee, Gollum. They sells it in bagginses.

No, no, no, precious, not the bagginses.

Give us three chances to order our coffee, master. Then we'll give it to you.

We're going to kill him, precious. He has his green apron and he wants it. He wants to take it from us.

No, no, no, Gollum, he'll give us the coffee, we don't need it.

Yes, precious, yes.

Please, master, please give us the precious.

Gollum hurls himself into the espresso machine. The shop grows quiet. Is that the sound of an eagle over-head? It must just be the wind.

A plump little fellow walks up to the counter. The barista looks down at him.

"Well, I'm back," he says.

Shakespeare

Mary Shelley goes up to the counter with her eccentric friend, who is wearing a lab coat. He wants to make his own drink out of the elements of other drinks: an espresso with hot chocolate, iced tea, whipped cream, caramel, pumpkin spice, mocha, and peppermint. "That's too many seasons at once!" the barista cries. There is a flash of lightning. The espresso machine begins to move. The back room of the Starbucks is full of pitchforks.

Deciding to wait out the angry mob that has begun following his wife, **Percy Bysshe Shelley** goes up to the counter and orders two Venti espressos. He sets them down on the table in front of him as if they are majestic stone pillars. He stands, knocks them to the ground dramatically, and leaves the shop. The barista hears his cries echo through the deserted street: "Look on my works, ye Mighty, and despair!"

Even after **Roberto Bolaño** leaves Starbucks, more and more orders pile up on the counter with his name written on them.

Cicero goes up to the counter and talks for seven hours about Rome and also a little bit about how he might want coffee.

Lydia Davis complains to her barista about how obscenely long Cicero's order took. She buys an espresso and downs it in one gulp.

Marius Pontmercy goes up to the counter and orders a coffee. He could afford an expensive Frappuccino, of course, but not everyone can, which isn't fair. All his friends are sitting at a table in the corner waiting for him to get his coffee so they can start their meeting, but he sees a pretty blond girl on the street outside and chases after her instead. When he finally gets back, he finds only empty chairs at an empty table.

Nathaniel Hawthorne comes in and orders a cappuccino. The barista spells his name without the "w." Hawthorne refuses to take the drink.

Herman Melville enters and orders a Trenta white chocolate mocha. Instead of waiting at the counter, he sits down at a table. The barista brings it over. "Don't you want to drink this, sir?" she asks. "I would prefer not to," says Melville. Before leaving, he steals Hawthorne's untouched drink off the counter and builds a shrine to it in his garage.

C. S. Lewis and **J. R. R. Tolkien** walk into the shop arm in arm.

Tolkien goes up to the counter and orders a Shaken Iced Blackberry Mojito Tea Lemonade. A group of hipsters in the drive-through lane overhear and immediately order the same thing, artfully photographing their drinks before tasting them. Tolkien is enraged and storms away, screaming about industrialization. C. S. Lewis calms him down with a piece of Turkish delight that he has inexplicably pulled from his jacket pocket, sits with Tolkien in the corner, and begins telling him all about County Down.

Tolkien is confused. Geography has never been his strong suit.

Tolkien's son has been paying close attention to Lewis; his map of Northern Ireland, scribbled on the back of a napkin, is flawless.

Aldous Huxley goes up to the counter and orders soma. The barista has no idea what that is and decides to ignore him. Huxley leaves the shop, grumbling under his breath about Deltas.

C. S. Lewis leaves with him.

W. H. Auden goes up to the counter and orders.

His drink is simple, a perfect drink for a chill day
in fall.

He has come to this shop after collecting his quarters

And has found that he has just enough money for a
Tall.

Why is he in this particular Starbucks? Where to
after this?

Though he drank so little coffee, he found that it
was bliss.

Emily Brontë goes up to the counter and orders a caffè latte. The barista misunderstands her and gives her a decaf cappuccino. Emily storms out in a fury, and spends the next decade walking past Starbucks carrying cups of Caribou Coffee. She and Starbucks never reconcile.

Charlotte Brontë goes up to the counter for a cup of tea and, Reader, she orders it!

Jane Eyre orders a Venti Earl Grey tea. It is raining outside. The barista is ugly and cold to her, but she falls in love with him anyway. There is a banging from the back room of the Starbucks, but the barista seems unconcerned. "It won't affect me bringing you your coffee," he assures Jane. He is wrong about this.

Charlotte catches **Jane**'s eye. "Hey, don't I know you?" she asks.

Wallace Stevens

I.

Among twenty Starbucks patrons
The only moving thing
Was the steam from the coffee.

II.

The barista was of three minds
Like an order
In which there are three coffees.

III.

The coffee steam whirled in the autumn winds.
It was a small part of the order.

IV.

A barista and a poet
Are one.
A barista, a poet, and a coffee
Are one.

V.

The barista did not know which to prefer
The beauty of lattes
Or the beauty of cappuccinos

The espresso machine whistling
Or just after.

VI.
Icicles filled the Starbucks window
With barbaric glass.
The shadow of the poet
Crossed it, to and fro.
His mood
Traced in the shadow
An indecipherable order.

VII.
O, thin patrons of Starbucks,
Why do you imagine eggnog lattes?
Do you not see how the black coffee
Waits on the counter
Of the baristas before you?

VIII.
The barista knows unpronounceable names
And complicated spellings
But she knows, too,
That the black coffee is involved
In what she knows.

IX.

When the coffee was placed on the counter
It marked the edge
Of one of many counters.

X.

At the sight of coffees black
Backlit by the green logo
Even the baristas of Starbucks
Would inhale sharply.

XI.

He came to Starbucks from Connecticut
Through the glass door.
Once, a fear pierced him
In that he mistook
Someone else's drink
For his own.

XII.

The machine is moving.
The coffee must be brewing.

XIII.

It was evening all afternoon.

It was snowing

And it was going to snow.

The black coffee sat

In the hands of Wallace Stevens.

Hans Castorp wants to leave Starbucks, but a barista talks him into sticking around. He figures he'll leave soon enough. And besides: He still has so much to learn from the other vaguely allegorical patrons!

Stephen King goes up to the counter and orders a Venti pumpkin spice latte. It's early afternoon in his small town in Maine, but shadows slip against the walls out of the corner of his eye. Someone coughs. A dog barks. A girl drinking coffee in the corner appears to be stirring her drink without touching it. There's a photo of King on the wall, but he's never been in this Starbucks before. He leaves and drops his coffee down the sewer. He doesn't hear it hit the ground.

Eugene O'Neill has relocated to the back corner and is heatedly debating with **James Joyce** as a horn sounds from outside.

James Joyce goes up to the counter and orders an Irish coffee no cream the barista tells him they don't serve alcoholic beverages here Joyce sighs and orders a black coffee and drinks it in the corner by the window as the snow falls down onto the cobblestones of the Irish town that the Starbucks is located in the barista comes over and asks if Joyce wants any sugar and he says yes I said yes I will yes.

Samuel Beckett goes to this same Starbucks—actually, never mind, it's in France.

Veronica Roth orders something delicious (and maybe quirky?), but before the baristas can complete her drink she leaves to go to a Starbucks in Chicago instead.

Truman Capote goes up to the counter and orders a caffé latte. As he pays for the drink, he accidentally drops the contents of his wallet on the counter. The barista looks down at the money and then up at Capote demurely.

"Hi there, stranger," she says. "My name is Holly."

"Trust me," says **Harper Lee**, suddenly appearing as if from nowhere. "You're barking up the wrong tree."

Jack Kerouac goes up to the counter but he doesn't really know what he wants to order, he hasn't thought about it much, he wasn't planning to come into this Starbucks except it was Dean's idea—isn't everything, in the end? Dean had had a hankering for Starbucks all day, was talking about it loudly as he drove over the speed limit on the dust road along the highway, pounding his fist on the wheel for emphasis, Kerouac laughing in the back, staring out the window thinking of that girl he had left that morning. He had thought she might have been the one, but when the morning light had come through the motel window he had realized they weren't meant to be, had gotten up and left before she'd even woken up. Now here he is waiting on line for coffee, remembering her, wondering where he'll be in the next ten years. Maybe at another Starbucks, in another town, with another woman on his arm, the sun setting low in the horizon and lighting up the dust and the dirt and the rocks and everyone in it, and he'll think of that Starbucks, and of **Dean Moriarty**, and even that coffee he ordered, and Dean Moriarty.

Tolkien, **Bradbury**, and **Emily Brontë** return to Starbucks with a lawsuit. They feel their work has been misrepresented! People have totally missed the point! This isn't what they intended at all! The baristas, terrified of litigation, are ready to give in when the doors of Starbucks are thrown open by none other than **Roland Barthes**. He delivers a passionate oration defending the interpretive rights of the reader.

Finding the litigants unmoved, Barthes grabs each author and, one at a time, forcefully ejects them from Starbucks.

"Thank you for clearing that up," says the barista. "What would you like? It's on the house." Barthes tells the barista that he's been desperate to try the Deconstructed Frappuccino ever since **Murakami** broke the news about Starbucks' secret menu.

He finds it greatly disappointing.

Willa Cather comes in and orders a blonde roast to go. She takes her travel cup and begins the long walk to the prairie. **Jack Kerouac** follows her, feeling slightly lost. By the time they reach the prairie, the coffee has gone cold, but it's a good kind of cold. The kind that reminds us of nature's authority. She sips it and gazes out at the countryside. The corn shudders under the setting sun. She's content. Kerouac doesn't understand who this woman is or why they're on a road trip if they're not going to sleep together.

Gabriel García Márquez goes up to the counter, orders an iced latte, and chats excitedly with the barista for about an hour. "Sorry I'm so talkative," he says. "I've been alone for what feels like a century."

Chichikov goes up to the counter and quietly asks the barista if he can buy empty paper cups. "Um," she says, "I guess so? But, like . . . why?" Chichikov starts to sweat. He mumbles an incoherent excuse before throwing money down on the counter, grabbing as many cups as he can carry, and running to his waiting troika. The barista is deeply curious about Chichikov, and hopes that there will be an opportunity for exposition later. Perhaps in a sequel.

Yossarian goes up to the counter to order a latte. He pulls out $3.00 to pay for it, but the barista informs him the price has recently gone up to $3.50. Yossarian has to run home to get fifty more cents, walking along a street full of murderers, rapists, child molesters; fires burning in every window, the acrid smell of smoke burning his nostrils. By the time he gets back, the price of a latte has been raised to $4.00.

The barista calls Eliot's name. **Yossarian** does a double take. "Did you say T. S. Eliot?" he repeats.

Terry Pratchett finally gets up to the counter after waiting in a queue that feels as though it's been moving at the pace of a giant turtle. "I'M SORRY, SIR," says his barista. "WERE YOU WAITING LONG? IT'S BEEN ONE HELL OF A DAY."

Billy Collins goes up to the counter at sunset
and orders a coffee, black, with cream.
It is warm, like childhood, like love, like losing
yourself in your art.
He holds the cup in his hands and stares across the
room.
There is a light on in the corner.
Underneath it is a woman, reading a book.
It is poetry. She is beautiful.
Why do we write? Because we want to get back to
that Starbucks,
In that corner, with that cup of coffee.
We want to be young again, and drinking coffee.
"Drink coffee with me," and she does.
She is beautiful. It is poetry.

Jane Austen looks up from her book to see a man
staring at her from across the Starbucks. Perturbed,
she goes up to the counter and orders a cinnamon
spice latte. The barista is a bore. The man at the table
in the corner orders exactly what she orders; he, too,
is a bore. He is handsome in the conventional sense,
but there is no chance they could ever be married.

Kurt Vonnegut goes up to the counter and orders an iced coffee. The barista, distracted by a monologue on the importance of basic kindness, accidentally adds ice-nine to the coffee instead of regular ice. She sets it down on the counter very carefully.

John Steinbeck goes up to the counter and begins to order, but sees that his barista's name is Adam. Steinbeck laughs and asks if he has any children. Adam just wants to get on with his day, so he says, "Can I take your order, sir?"

Steinbeck says, "Thou mayest."

Pablo Neruda goes up to the counter.
The air in the shop is sultry sweet;
The barista is beautiful, sensuous, warm—
A caramel macchiato with eyes like stars.
She has a flower behind her ear.
She gives him a cup of tea.
Moonlight streams in from the windows.
He could stay here forever,
Drinking his tea,
Making love to his barista.

Billy Collins exits in a huff.

Flannery O'Connor goes up to the counter, but before she gets there she has a horrible thought—the Starbucks she had been meaning to go to was in Tennessee! This Starbucks is populated with myriad locals, all of whom eye the unwelcome visitor warily. O'Connor orders an Americano. She doesn't care for the taste. A good coffee, after all, is hard to find.

D. H. Lawrence goes up to the counter and orders from the secret menu. This decision immediately isolates him from the other patrons of Starbucks, and he seats himself far away from them by choice.

Gregor Samsa goes up to the counter and tries to order a black coffee. Everyone runs screaming from the room.

Atticus Finch goes up to the counter and orders the one drink on the menu that no one else was brave enough to get. Waiting for his coffee, he tells the patrons of Starbucks they were too hasty in their judgment of **Gregor**: "Never judge a man until you've considered things from his point of view." As he walks out, the patrons stand up in solidarity.

The Bennet sisters come into Starbucks with their mother.

Jane Bennet goes up to the counter to order and is immediately surrounded by male patrons trying to guess her drink of choice. She demurs, casting anxious glances at her sisters, while her mother attempts to corral the gentlemen. "Whoever wants to buy you the most expensive drink, that's the one you let order for you," she tells Jane. "Let me handle this."

Elizabeth Bennet goes up to the counter and orders off the secret menu, because fuck convention.

Lydia Bennet goes up to the counter and tries to order whatever Lizzie just ordered, but she is unfamiliar with the secret menu, so she just gets a Strawberries & Crème Frappuccino. She's off caffeine.

Kitty Bennet says, "Make that order a double." The barista writes "Lydia" on both cups.

Mary Bennet goes up to the counter and orders a small coffee. She does not sit with her family.

James Bond goes up to the counter and orders a martini. The barista is confused, but finds his manly audacity attractive. Later, the two sleep together. Afterward, Bond says: "I've always loved a fresh roast!"

"That doesn't even make sense," whispers the barista.

Anna Karenina orders chai, but changes her mind when she sees someone walk past with a Frappuccino.

John Green goes up to the counter and orders an espresso shot. The barista gives him a Venti caffé espresso Frappuccino. Green says, "This isn't what I ordered." The barista replies, "You ordered a drizzle, I'm giving you a hurricane."

Donald Barthelme goes up to the counter. He is very nervous. He wants to order that which will impress the barista. He wants a chance to slip his hands under her clothing, so he will order something to impress, because that is definitely the best way to go about seduction. He orders a Frapuccino, pronouncing the word like a confession of adoration. It does not work. This is his third attempt today. He throws away this Frapuccino, like all the others.

Hannibal Lecter enters the Starbucks. He greets the barista with an unwarranted amount of eye contact. Lecter sits without ordering; he's brought his own little sandwich. The barista hopes that it's roast beef, but doesn't look too closely.

Titus Andronicus enters Starbucks with his daughter **Lavinia.** He places an order for each of them, though it's clear from her grunting that perhaps Titus isn't very good at understanding what his daughter wants. Titus and Lavinia share a table with **Hannibal Lecter,** who offers them some of his sandwich.

William Carlos Williams

orders shaken iced

tea lemonade.

It is delicious

so sweet

and so cold.

Aram Saroyan

It's getting late, so **You** and **The Lyric "I"** leave Starbucks, walking awful close together.

Laura Ingalls Wilder goes up to the counter and orders a small cup of extra hot coffee. She sits down at a table in the Starbucks she has built for herself out of elm from the prairie. She writes a letter to her family. It's going to be a long winter.

Christopher Marlowe goes up to the counter and begins ordering a coffee but, before he can finish, he is stabbed to death by **Hannibal Lecter**. No one will ever know what he was going to order, but some say it would have been better than what **Shakespeare** ordered.

Hannibal is taken from Starbucks by the police.

William Goldman goes up to the counter and orders a large chocolate chai. "As you wish," says the barista.

Geoffrey Chaucer staggers into the Starbucks, leading twenty-four others, all of whom seem on the brink of collapse. "Twenty-five large coffees," he says. "It's been a long trip."

Chaucer

William Goldman's drink is ready, but the barista refuses to give it to him. She insists that the drink was made for S. Morgenstern.

"This isn't fair!" Goldman says.

The barista smiles and shakes her head. "Who says life is fair?"

Horatio comes into Starbucks with **Bernardo** and **Marcellus**. They all want to split a Venti white chocolate mocha, and decide amongst themselves that since Horatio is the only one who went to college, he should do the actual ordering. Horatio orders. When he turns around, everyone else in the Starbucks is dead.

Hamlet's coffee order sits on the counter untouched.

George R. R. Martin enters. Upon seeing the carnage, he grins. "Niiice," he says.

The baristas close the shop for twenty minutes to drag all the bodies out the back door.

George R. R. Martin takes over behind the counter as the baristas clean up. For his first customer, he prepares an intricate and tantalizing drink. Martin calls the customer up to the counter, then lets them watch as he slowly pours their drink onto the floor.

Three well-dressed, swashbuckling men sashay up to the counter and order three Grande espressos. Five minutes later, a panting **D'Artagnan**, wearing similar (although less authentic) clothing, runs up to the counter and demands to be served the same thing as the three who just entered. He insists that he is the fourth member of their group, but the barista refuses to acknowledge him, especially as he had been in earlier in the day without his supposed companions.

The Brothers Grimm go up to the counter and order two hazelnut macchiatos. They sit in a corner and chat up every person who walks by their table, taking copious notes on their conversations. Their coffees seem blacker than most people remember them.

Hans Christian Andersen orders a white chocolate mocha Frappuccino. His coffee is too cold and he cries, overwhelmed at the hardships he has faced. Then he remembers he's a successful author and cheers up immediately. He buys coffees for everyone in the Starbucks. A bell rings in the distance, probably celebrating his good deeds.

Helen Oyeyemi asks the barista for an empty cup. She snatches drinks from the Grimms and Hans Christian Andersen, mixes them up, and shotguns them. She bows, and exits the Starbucks with decidedly more pep in her step.

Gandalf goes up to the counter just as the barista is having a nervous breakdown. "People are dying left and right!" she cries. "Couldn't you have come sooner?"

"Actually, no," says Gandalf.

Aslan goes up to the counter and orders a Venti steamed milk. He leaves, comes back three days later, and drinks it. "That's kind of a heavy-handed metaphor," notes the barista.

Gandalf asks **Aslan** for his autograph.

Agatha Christie arrives on the scene to investigate the death of **Christopher Marlowe.** While in Starbucks, she learns that **Chaucer**'s pilgrims have all gone missing. A confused **Horatio** talks to her for a little while, but doesn't understand how he could be a suspect. She stirs her caffé mocha dramatically. Agatha Christie turns to the other occupants of the Starbucks and announces that she knows who has committed the murder. One barista attempts to escape without notice, but a disguised policeman subdues her quickly. Christie looks down, but her coffee is missing. It reappears a week later. No one has ever determined where it went for those seven days.

Rosencrantz and Guildenstern go up to the counter, hoping to order Venti caffé lattes. The barista, whose name tag reads only "The Bard," gives them Talls and tells them to drink their coffee quickly and leave the store. The two friends begin drinking just as The Bard's shift ends. The new barista, whose name tag reads "**Tom**," sits down, puts his arms around Rosencrantz and Guildenstern, and gives them the biggest drinks they've ever seen in their lives.

"Tell me all about your days," says Tom.

Horatio grumbles under his breath.

Edward Gorey goes up to the counter and orders a Venti cappuccino. There is a sicklysweet scent in the air. Basil and Clarence are playing charades, although Maude appears to be winning. Gorey grows suspicious of the mustachioed man in the corner, who has been writing a long list for the past several minutes. He exits the shop and heads for the train tracks. Perhaps the man who is chasing him will grow tired.

Edward had become increasingly convinced that the barista intended to do away with him.

Jeffrey Eugenides goes up to the counter and orders five white chocolate mochas. A group of boys watches him from outside the Starbucks. They observe as he drinks each drink one by one, throws the cups out one by one, and exits the Starbucks, walking away down the street until they can't see him anymore.

Nancy Drew calmly strolls up to the counter, orders a stiff drink, and relaxes in the corner while poring over what appears to be an ancient book. Twenty minutes later, the **Hardy Boys** run breathlessly into the shop, rejoicing at their physical fortitude and apparent genius at having solved yet another alliterative mystery: the Location of the Lost Latte Lagoon. The barista points over to Nancy Drew, who tips her glass to the two sweaty gentlemen and nonchalantly goes back to her book. She high-fives **Agatha Christie** on the way out.

"We're still on for drinks tomorrow night, right?" says Agatha.

William Blake goes up to the counter and orders a Venti raspberry lemonade and the biggest scone he sees, claiming they are both "for a friend." There is no one with him, and so the barista assumes that Blake is buying them for one of his imaginary angels. He serves Blake anyway, figuring that it doesn't really matter if the drinker is a hallucination so long as the money is real. Blake surprises him by leaving the café and giving the food to a hungry boy on the street corner.

Margaret Atwood goes up to the counter, but the Starbucks is no longer serving coffee. In fact, coffee has ceased to be manufactured. Atwood recalls the taste of coffee—sweet and bitter, a little melancholy— but she can't quite recreate it perfectly. It's gone, like the world she once knew, a whisper on the winds across the unknowable ocean. She leaves the Starbucks. The streets are empty. Her footsteps echo as she crosses the pavement, heads out of the city into fields, which brush against her body as she moves through them. She can nearly see the ocean. She gets into a van that will take her to somewhere.

John McPhee only came into Starbucks for an orange; he seems shocked by the sudden coalescence of a four-course meal in front of him. None of the other patrons even pretends to be surprised.

Patroclus goes up to the counter and orders **Achilles'** drink for him because he refuses to do it himself. The barista makes the coffee too hot. It burns Patroclus. When **Achilles** finds out he storms in and throws the rest of the coffee at the barista, who peels off his apron and quits in frustration.

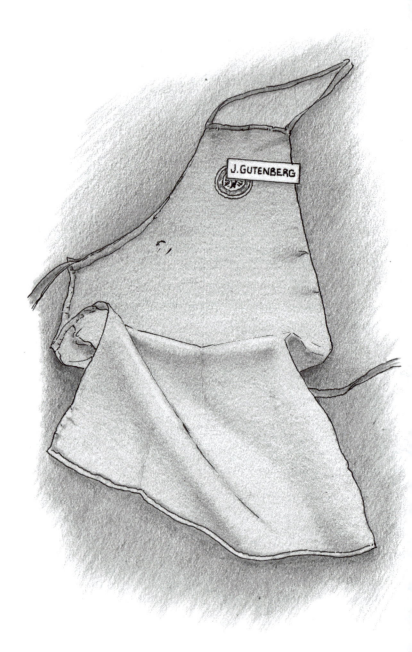

Achilles is spurred to organize a protest outside the Starbucks due to the multiple customers that have been burned throughout the day. He is joined by **Daisy Miller, Icarus,** and **Brett Easton Ellis**, who doesn't know what the protest is about. He just enjoys protesting capitalism.

Kazuo Ishiguro goes up to the counter nearly a decade since his last Starbucks visit and orders a green tea latte. It's nothing like the last drink he ordered. Then again, none of the drinks he ordered are truly similar, but they are all delicious.

Jay Gatsby goes up to the counter and orders a Starbucks Vanilla Iced Coffee, but only after being repeatedly reassured by his companion that it is a sufficiently aristocratic choice. While waiting, Gatsby daydreams about his choice: the delicate balance of bitter and sweet; the refreshing chill on this humid summer day; the way sunlight will refract in the swirling liquid. It is, he decides, a flawless and thoroughly American choice of beverage. Gatsby does not know that Starbucks Vanilla Iced Coffee is premade and served in a bottle. He is hurt and confused.

His companion, **Romeo,** orders a white chocolate mocha. As he's waiting for it, the barista sets down a hazelnut macchiato for someone else. Romeo is struck by the realization that this is the perfect drink for him, and takes it, forgetting that he and everyone in his family is allergic to nuts.

Both men exit the shop together. The baristas draw the blinds behind them. They have a bad feeling about those guys.

Sophocles goes up to the counter and orders an incredibly complex drink with interwoven ingredients and various flavored syrups. Understandably, the barista messes up his order. Sophocles blames her for the shop's downfall and banishes her to a windowless room in the basement.

The three remaining baristas huddle together and decide that if they're going to survive this bloodbath, they're going to have to work together.

Lady Macbeth goes up to the counter and sees three female baristas intently hovering over the espresso machine, chanting something unintelligible. She decides to order a Passion tea and proceeds to spill it all over her clothes and hands. She runs screaming to the bathroom. The three baristas cackle in uncanny unison.

Mr. Darcy goes up to the counter and orders a caramel flan latte. He drinks it and is displeased. Then again, he has only had half a dozen acceptable Starbucks drinks in his life.

John Updike goes up to the counter and orders a caffè Americano. The barista draws a rabbit on the cup. He drinks it slowly, over many hours. When he finishes, he writes out a review and drops it into a feedback box.

The barista looks at the clock she is so bored she has been here most of the day and wants to go home how much longer does she have—another hour seriously? An older guy is walking up to the counter now what is he gonna order something simple probably hopefully. "What can I get for you today?" she asks. "I'll have a flat white," says **William Faulkner**.

John Updike watches the man come in toward the end of the day as the light is fading through the windows of the immaculate coffee shop. He is gentlemanly and he walks with purpose; he looks world-weary. Updike thinks that he would like to have coffee with this man. He feels a certain solidarity with him.

Mr. Darcy notices another gentleman enter the shop and he is duly impressed with the apparent class of this man who is nowhere near as shoddily dressed as some of the other patrons of this shop, and perhaps he hasn't chosen such a dowdy establishment after all, and he internally praises himself for yet another turn of good judgment but, to be fair, he is very often right in these matters, and in most matters.

We in the Starbucks noticed the man come in, but we watch a lot of people come in. We've watched everyone come in throughout the day, and while this man certainly had an air of importance about him, so have many people who have passed through those heavy glass doors throughout this day and days past, and probably will in days future. We'll listen to his drink order and we'll make it, sure, but will we remember it?

William Faulkner goes up to the counter and orders a flat white. Even though he is far from home, he is comforted by the fact that this Starbucks is identical to the one in Yoknapatawpha country. In fact, as he looks around he feels that he recognizes many familiar faces, collected throughout the vast and varied experiences of his long life. He turns to the woman behind him and smiles. Surely he knows her as well. These other patrons of Starbucks have lives hidden away inside of them, think things he can only guess at, and know things he may never know. He picks up his drink. This coffee, his order, is a record of his heart, a universal truth, that one day, he stood in this Starbucks and he ordered a flat white.

Jennifer Egan orders myriad drinks for various patrons of the Starbucks, all of whom are tenuously connected to one another, including herself and **William Faulkner,** who once met at a party in New York many years ago. They take a selfie. She live-tweets her entire Starbucks experience.

Worlds collide! Drinking coffee with @WilliamFaulkner at #Starbucks

Dylan Thomas enters the completely empty shop and orders nineteen carefully crafted, ten-syllable coffees. In the time he has taken to recite his order, the motion-sensor-operated lights have turned off and the entire shop has plunged into murky darkness. No one hears his order and he rages, rages against the dying of the light. **John Steinbeck** is out in the parking lot unionizing the baristas.

VLADIMIR: He didn't say for sure he'd come.

ESTRAGON: And if he doesn't come?

VLADIMIR: We'll come back tomorrow.

ESTRAGON: And then the day after tomorrow.

VLADIMIR: Possibly.

ESTRAGON: And so on.

VLADIMIR: The point is—

ESTRAGON: Until he comes.

VLADIMIR: You're merciless.

George Saunders orders an XPressOXtreme from the CoffeElator in the corner. Something about the drink seems familiar, but it's darker than usual coffee. Saunders takes it to go.

H. D. goes up to the counter;
she orders a brimming cup
of whatever is the special for today.
A slow sip, a quick look.
The Greeks would certainly
have something to say about this.
She turns quickly away
and resumes reading her book.

J.K. Rowling goes up to the counter and orders seven pumpkin spice lattes. The barista gives her eight.

Jorge Luis Borges goes up to the counter. He comes to the conclusion that the possible permutations of size, flavor, and strength stretch far beyond what any one man could experience. He orders every permutation and moves to the back of the room, where he will spend the rest of his days attempting to catalog all the possibilities of the infinite Starbucks menu.

Tennessee Williams goes up to the counter and orders a coffee, but he doesn't pay for it himself. He always depends on the kindness of strangers.

As the baristas begin to close up shop, **Eugene O'Neill** finishes the dregs of his drink and walks off into the foggy night. A horn sounds in the distance.

It has grown dark outside. The streetlamps are beginning to turn on. The baristas are exhausted.

Lemony Snicket goes up to the counter and orders a caffé Americano. It is bitter. The barista is armed. The man in the corner has poisoned someone's drink. The espresso machine is on fire. Lemony Snicket begins to run down the street as the Starbucks explodes. He is being chased. He spills his coffee.

Ahab goes up to the smoldering counter and orders a white chocolate mocha. He stares at the barista intently.

"Make it the biggest one you have, lad," he says saltily.

"I can give you a Trenta," the barista meekly replies.

"No!" Ahab cries. "Give me whatever's the biggest. I need it!"

The barista quietly talks to his manager, and they begin turning on every nozzle on the espresso machine.

"It'll just be a few minutes, sir," the manager says.

"I can wait," says Ahab. "I've been waiting years for this drink."

Finally, the barista and the manager take Ahab behind the shop and show him the dumpster, full to the brim with steaming hot coffee.

"That's more like it," Ahab says, sticking a coffee stirrer into the drink.

He is pulled down into the mocha abyss, along with the manager and the rest of the store. Only the barista remains, holding for dear life on to a single coffee-cup sleeve, crying out for help.

EPILOGUE

Nineteen Years Later

Rip Van Winkle wakes up, confused but unhurt. He yawns, stretches his back, and strolls around the block to another Starbucks.

ABOUT THE AUTHORS

Jill Poskanzer goes up to the counter and deliberates for a solid minute before ordering a tall white chocolate mocha, which is what she always orders. She just enjoys the illusion of change, not the practical concept. She currently lives in Los Angeles, where she's pursuing a career writing for television. You can follow her at @MsJillMadeline on Twitter.

Wilson Josephson goes up to the counter and orders a large hot chocolate, but he forgets about it, and by the time he gets around to drinking it, it's cold. He revels in amateurism in all things and firmly believes that suckin' at something is the first step toward being sorta good at something. He is pursuing a career.

Nora Katz goes up to the counter and orders whatever Tolkien orders. When she's not performing or hiking or designing her dream home in the Shire, she is pursuing a career as a historian and museum curator.